NORTHERN CALIFORNIA
LAND OF MANY DREAMS

Text by
Bill Harris

Designed & Produced by
TED SMART and **DAVID GIBBON**

CRESCENT BOOKS
NEW YORK

Featuring the Photography of Neil Sutherland
CLB 856
© 1985 Illustrations and text: Colour Library Books Ltd.,
Guildford, Surrey, England.
Text filmsetting by Acesetters Ltd., Richmond, Surrey, England.
Printed in Spain.
All rights reserved.
1985 edition published by Crescent Books, distributed by Crown Publishers, Inc.
ISBN 0 517 478099
h g f e d c b a

The year was 1848 and James Marshall was tired. He had been building a sawmill for John Sutter on the American River, but it wasn't going particularly well. And then, as he stood on the bank of the river staring into the water, he noticed something so shiny that he reached down to pick it up. He'd never seen anything like it. It was rough and hard and glittered gaily in the sun.

He took the pebble down to Sutter and they "applied every test of their ingenuity and the American Encyclopedia," and Eureka! They had found it. The gold strike was on.

Eureka! became the password of Alta (upper) California. Folks named the pretty little town on the Redwood coast Eureka and they made it their state motto and put it on their state seal. That one word said it all. I have found it!

Californians are a pretty smug lot. They know they found a lot more than gold that day in 1848. They found some of the most spectacular natural scenery anywhere in the world. From the jagged, rocky cliffs of California's coast, to the placid rivers and streams that wind through the gold rush country, to the waterfalls that plummet from mammoth granite cliffs with a roar to the distant valley floor below in Yosemite Park, to the snowy-peaked point of Mt. Shasta, Northern California is a land of awesome beauty.

But there's no doubt about it. Somebody up there simply made a mistake when they glued Northern and Southern California together. They might as well be two different countries. Along the West Coast, the sunny beaches give way to sharp, steep cliffs and a rocky coastline just above San Luis Obispo. On the Eastern boundary, the parched desert of Death Valley is transformed into the Sequoia National Park in the space of a miracle. If you were to stand at Dante's View you could see Mt. Whitney, the highest mountain peak in the continental United States and at the same time look down to the lowest point in the hemisphere – a mere 3 miles away.

As with any wonder of nature, though, there is a reason for all this diversity. As many as 200 million years ago California simply didn't exist. The country that would one day become the United States ended in present-day Nevada, with a coastline similar to California's. Over the years basalt and

lava pushed upward, sometimes erupting in the form of volcanoes and occasionally breaking the surface of the water.

Bit by bit the coastline pushed westward, eventually forming the Sierra Mountain Range. At some point, probably about 140 million years ago, the Northern half of the Sierras broke off and moved westward, forming the Klamath Range.

Meanwhile, basalt and lava were continuing their activity at sea. When the Sierras quietened down, another smaller mountain range pushed its head above the water. This would become the Coast Range, running just north of San Francisco to the California border. Between the Sierras and the Coast Range ran a giant 450-mile lake. Eventually, that filled with sediment to form California's rich Central Valley.

Through the centuries, volcanoes, glaciers, rivers and ocean activity have worked to form Northern California. Geologists thought the volcanic activity had ended until they were surprised in 1980 by Mt. St. Helens' eruption. Although that's in the Cascade Range to the north, they're paying much more attention now to the Sierra Range, and Lassen Volcanic National Park is a continuously bubbling reminder of the unrest just below the surface.

Both the Sierras and the Klamaths are today thickly forested and dense with vegetation. They're a backpacker's paradise, with few roads and an abundance of wildlife, wildflowers and serene quiet, but the serenity above ground deceptively belies the constantly changing tensions just below the surface.

People who choose to live in Northern California are as diverse as their landscape. From the super-achievers who live in high-tech Silicon Valley to the lumberjacks who live in the Sierras and Redwood country, Northern California has it all. California is our most populous state with 23,500,000 residents. That tops the next state in the scale, New York, by some 6,000,000 people.

California was founded on a myth and the myth was gold. It started as early as 1540. Spain was at the height of her explorations, and was searching distant lands for gold. In 1542

King Philip II sent one of his most trusted navigators, Juan Rodriguez Cabrillo, to take a look around. Cabrillo saw very little to impress him, but he did take the time to claim all the land for Spain.

Cabrillo was definitely not impressed by the few Indians he found. These Indians had, centuries earlier, crossed the land bridge at the Bering Strait, filtered down through Alaska and Canada and finally found their way to Northern California. Their land provided them with abundant crops, a surplus of fish, birds and animals to hunt, and a relaxed, quiet way of life. They remained close to home, where their easy, tranquil life had provided amply for them for over 1000 years.

The Spanish claim to the land didn't impress the Indians in the least. If they had taken any notice of the Spaniard's peculiar behavior, they must merely have thought they were performing some strange religious ceremony.

The English explorer, Sir Francis Drake, didn't pay much attention to the Spanish claim either. In 1579 Drake and his crew on the *Golden Hind* had been having a great time running up and down the California and Mexico coasts pillaging and ransacking the Spanish towns. They stole silver, gold, spices and furs for their Queen in England. When Drake reached San Francisco Bay he didn't let a little thing like a prior Spanish claim worry him. Instead, he claimed the area for "Queen Elizabeth and Her Successors Forever."

Drake was a dandy. One prisoner reported that: "He is served on silver dishes with gold borders and gilded garlands in which are his arms and he carries all possible dainties and perfumed waters."

Drake loaded his ship with furs, took on a treasure of spice in the Moluccas, and returned to England in 1580. There, a pleased Queen Elizabeth knighted him for his exploits. But this was a mere preview of England's colonization. The colonies still belonged to Spain. Besides, Spain was still looking for that elusive gold.

For some reason lost to historians, mapmakers had moved the location of the mythical city of Quivira from a spot in Kansas reported by Coronado in 1540, to a place on the California Coast near Cape Mendocino. It was pure fantasy, of course, but legends die hard. So, as late as 1603, King Philip of Spain sent a navigator up the coast. Padre Ascension, who traveled along on this trip, wrote:

"Philip III found among his father's secret papers a sworn declaration that some foreigners had given him in which it is stated that they had seen and discovered some notable things, on passing through the Strait of Anian, where they were driven in a ship by the great force of continual winds. In this they relate how they passed from the North Sea to the South Sea by this strait, and that, while searching for shelter from the storm, they entered a copious river, on which they came in sight of a populous and rich city named Quivira, well filled with civilised, courteous and very literate people wearing clothes, and well fortified and surrounded by a wall."

On this trip they found nothing to recommend to the folks back home. In fact, it was a dismal disappointment. They encountered fog and wind and bitter cold. They found no grand city, merely a few huts occupied by the local Indians. Worst of all, they found no gold. As far as we know, that was the last time a Spanish vessel visited the Northern California coast. In fact, the Spanish didn't even bother to plant a flag until 1769.

Actually, the Spanish had another important mission in life besides looking for gold. They wanted to save souls. Wherever they found humans untrained in the ways of Christ, they assumed that responsibility. It was the missionaries who came to California and left the most lasting Spanish heritage.

The year was 1769. On the other side of the continent, the English were firmly entrenched and in control. A few years later, political unrest would grow to such an extent that a Revolutionary War would take place. But on the West Coast, the Indian's tranquil life was much the same as it had been 1000 years earlier.

Spain's international dominion was on the wane. England's was on the rise. The Jesuits had just been expelled from Mexico, so their establishments in Baja (lower) California were turned over to the Franciscans, under the leadership of Father Junipero Serra. Spain decided the time had come to expand north to Alta (upper) California. What better way to do so than to establish religious missions to care for the spiritual needs of the heathens?

Father Serra himself led the missionary expedition, and on July 16, 1769 established the first of 21 missions. It was located in San Diego, but he continued up the coast, establishing, in 1770, a mission in Monterey. Finally, in 1776, Father Serra founded a mission "on the port of our father, San Francisco." He wrote that if the site "could be well settled like Europe there would be nothing more beautiful in the world."

The next day Father Serra established yet another mission just three miles to the southeast. Mission Dolores, now located in a populous section of downtown San Francisco, is today a serene oasis in a bustling city. With its quiet gardens, splashing fountains and cool interior, it remains San Francisco's only link with its colonial past.

The mission system, which had proved successful in Mexico and Baja California, rested on three legs: the mission, the pueblo and the presidio. The mission saw to the religious needs of the community. The pueblo was the civil leg and consisted of plots of land for homes, gardens and common grazing land. The presidio was the military leg, made up of a fort or garrison. Its purpose was to protect the fledgling towns from attack.

Father Serra established a presidio in San Francisco. It remains as the headquarters of the U.S. Sixth Army. With its manicured lawns, golf course, lake and breathtaking views over the Pacific Ocean, it ranks on every soldier's list as number one duty – right next to heaven itself.

As pure as the Spanish motives might have been, Spain's treatment of their Indian charges was less than beneficial. A Russian captain visiting the Bay in 1816 reported: "The uncleanliness of these barracks (missions) baffles description and is perhaps the cause of the great mortality, for of 1,000 Indians at San Francisco, 300 die each year."

Worse was the Spanish insistence that the Indians be removed from their land. The Captain continued; "Twice in a year they receive permission to return to their homes. This short time is the happiest of their existence, and I myself have seen them going home in crowds with loud rejoicings. The sick, who cannot undertake the journey, at least accompany their happy countrymen to the shore where they embark, and there sit for days, together mournfully gazing on the distant summits of the mountains which surround their homes. They often sit in the posture for several days, without taking any food, so much does the sight of their lost home affect these new Christians. Every time, some of those who have permission run away and they would probably all do it, were they not deterred by their fear of the soldiers, who catch them and bring them back to the Mission as criminals."

The Spanish remained in control of California until one day in 1824 when Mexico simply declared itself a republic and independent from Spain. But, lacking resources to take a firm grasp on those lands to the north, Mexico started a new policy. They opened California up to colonization. Promises of huge grants of free land (the average was nearly 23,000 acres) sent settlers north. Still, they were mostly cattle ranchers. Building cities was not their interest.

Cattle ranching was an easy life. The weather was mild and the grasses thick. Clear, sunny skies beamed down on the hills and valleys.

In 1826 Jedediah Smith made the first overland trip to California. Others were not far behind. Joseph Walker came in 1833, followed by Captain John C. Fremont, Kit Carson and others. These new folks consisted of a ragtag group who were feisty and stubborn.

Yerba Buena Cove (later to be called San Francisco) was described in 1834 by one visitor as a village of perhaps 200 people – Yankees, Mexicans, Dutch, Indians and a few folks from the Sandwich Islands – who "lived and loved together, and their eternal routine of drinking, smoking and dancing was never interrupted save by an occasional rodeo kicked up by the wild boys of the ranches, the periodical visitations of hide-doggers, or the rare appearance of a man-of-war or whale ship in the harbor."

In 1835, the writer Richard Henry Dana was to arrive by ship in Yerba Buena Cove. In his book *Two Years Before the Mast*, he described the Bay's "large and beautifully wooded islands... the abundance of water, the extreme fertility of its shores, the excellence of its climate, which is as near as being perfect as any in the world..."

The village he found consisted of merely one shanty of rough boards. The Presidio had already been deserted and Mission Dolores had no full-time priest. He was to note tremendous changes as time went by.

Five years later life in Yerba Buena Cove was described by Julia Cooley Altrocchi in her book *Spectacular Californians*, as a "joyous beautiful life" that "moved like a carousel all around the prosaic American settlement." But the village itself was still no more than a collection of shacks situated on a dingy mudflat.

As early as 1835, President Andrew Jackson had offered Mexico a sum of $500,000 for the purchase of California. Mexico refused. Nevertheless, it was becoming apparent to Mexico that they were experiencing an invasion of sorts. Governor Paco Pico said: "We find ourselves threatened by hordes of Yankee emigrants whose progress we cannot arrest."

Mexico had reason to worry. The United States government really did want California and New Mexico for itself. By 1845 President James Polk had an emissary in Mexico offering to buy the land for as much as $40 million, if necessary. The negotiations were unsuccessful, however, and on May 13, 1846, President Polk declared war on Mexico.

War didn't affect Northern California much. It effectively ended on July 9, 1846, less than two months after it began, when 70 sailors and marines marched ashore in Yerba Buena Cove and raised the stars and stripes. By the time the war officially ended in February 1848, Northern California had already settled into a comfortable routine of American rule. They had even taken on a new name. On January 30, 1847. Yerba Buena Cove was officially renamed San Francisco.

Through all the hostilities, the little village of San Francisco remained a sluggish outpost of civilization, inhabited by a mere 600 souls. But all that was about to change.

The story of California is the story of gold. And in 1848 James W. Marshall struck the first traces of that elusive metal that had been the quest of men for centuries.

Actually, if John Augustus Sutter had not been a screwball, Marshall might not have made his find. Sutter was born in Switzerland in 1803. He arrived in the United States via the Hawaiian Islands, where it's rumored that he lost a great deal of money entrusted to him in a trade scheme. Anyway, he arrived in San Francisco in 1839. His occupations, he announced, were former Swiss Army officer and dry goods merchant, but those didn't interest him much anymore.

He had heard of the large land grants being offeed by the Mexicans, and he somehow convinced them that he should have not one, but two. The authorities gave him a total of 50,000 acres of the rich Central Valley land right between the Sierra Nevada Mountain Range and the Coast Range. One of the first things he did was to establish Fort Sutter, at the precise spot where Sacramento now stands. It was the first stop for the weary and bedraggled folks who had trekked overland across the Sierra Nevadas on their way to the Coast. Sutter gave them a warm bed and hot meals and a bath – all at a price.

Sutter's greatest problem was that his dreams were always bigger than his capacity for seeing them through, and he had an appalling appetite for credit at ruinous rates of interest.

He planted wheat and fruit orchards on his land and in 1847 he decided to build a sawmill on the American River. Most people thought this was a crazy idea. John Bidwell, an early emigrant, wrote: "Rafting sawed lumber down the canyons of the American River (was such a) wild scheme that no other man than Sutter would have been confiding and credulous to believe it possible."

Sutter hired Marshall to build the mill. One day Marshall let all the water out of the dam behind the mill in order to enlarge the channel. The next day he looked into the millrace and couldn't believe his eyes. There were shiny bits of metal tumbling gaily down the river and lodged in the new-found riverbank. He was sure it must be gold. The date was January 24, 1848.

Marshall took some nuggets to Sutter and together they looked in all the books they could find. Sure enough! It was gold. They raced back to the mill and gathered up some more.

Sutter wrote an account of this historic day. "'Do you know,' said Mr. Marshall to me, 'I positively debated within myself two or three times whether I should take the trouble to bend my back to pick up one of the pieces and had decided on not doing so when further on another glittering morsel caught my eye – the largest of the pieces now before you. I condescended to pick it up, and to my astonishment found that it was a thin scale of what appears to be pure gold!' He then gathered some twenty or thirty pieces which on examination convinced him that his suppositions were right. His first impression was that this gold had been lost or buried there by some early Indian tribe – perhaps some of those mysterious inhabitants of the west of whom we have no account but who dwelt on this continent centuries ago, and built those cities and temples, the ruins of which are scattered about these solitary wilds. On proceeding, however, to examine the neighbouring soil, he discovered that it was more or less auriferous. This at once decided him. He mounted his horse and rode down to me as fast as it could carry him with the news."

Sutter's Fort was an impossible place to keep a secret. Soon word had spread to San Francisco. It's said that on May 12th, Sam Brannan, owner of the *California Star* walked through the streets of San Francisco holding a vial of gold dust and shouting "Gold! Gold! Gold on the American River!"

Eureka! They had found it! San Francisco emptied overnight. Prospectors cleaned out stores selling axes, tents, crackers, picks, pans and any other necessity for living in the wilderness and gathering riches. Monterey, Oregon Territory, San Jose and Eureka all joined in the frantic scramble for gold.

Word reached Washington of the gold strike. President Polk announced the discovery to Congress. Soon the *New York Herald* wrote: "The El Dorado of the old Spaniards is discovered at last."

In the first three years of the gold rush more than 200,000 people came to California in one of the greatest mass migrations in history. They came to a land they knew little about. They were called "The forty-niners" and they were plucky and young. Mostly farm boys, bored clerks or adventurers – over half were in their twenties.

Tales of California were abundant but, for the most part, pure fantasy. Prentice Mulford of Sag Harbor, New York remembered the tales he heard in school: "California was but a blotch of yellow on the schoolboy's map... The Sacramento River was reported as abounding in alligators... The general opinion was that it was a fearfully hot country and full of snakes." That didn't keep them from coming. Not even Mulford.

About half of the forty-niners came overland, picking up supplies and provisions either in St. Joseph, St. Louis or Independence, Missouri. They teamed up with other gold seekers for the long trek west and generally followed the shallow, weaving Platt River through Nebraska, crossing the Rockies at South Pass. They would stock up again at the Mormon capital of Salt Lake City and head across the Great Basin. Cholera was their worst enemy, but Indian attacks were a constant fear as well.

The World Health Organization, commenting on the treatment of cholera in the United States in 1850 said: "Your chances of surviving an attack were about as good as though you had been shot in the stomach at point blank range... maybe fifty percent. On the other hand, if you fell into the hands of the average doctor, your chances of dying rose to about ninety percent."

In other words, casualties were high. It wasn't much better on the sea route, however. It was quickest to go by way of Panama. Ships crammed with forty-niners sailed to the port of Aspinwall. From there they went by canoe, mule and on foot across the Isthmus. On the other side, they found the town of Panama, where the adventurers bid madly for the first ship to San Francisco.

The overland route took five to six months of backbreaking work. The Panama route could be accomplished in the relatively fast time of six to eight weeks. Little wonder they put up with the hardships of crossing the Isthmus to reach the gold faster.

Those who were lucky enough to make it were often rewarded. In 1849 $10 million worth of gold was mined in California and in 1850 four times that. In the first seven years alone, a total of $450 million of gold was taken out of the hills of the Mother Lode.

Out of necessity, most miners worked alone. Claims were limited to the ground a man could actually work. Most of the early miners were untrained and used unsophisticated methods. They let the rushing streams do most of the work. They would stand or squat beside the tumbling waters, capturing a panful of gravel which they sifted through, looking for the elusive gold. Later, as technology improved, mine operators drilled shafts to dig the gold out of the solid rock.

Most of the forty-niners were adventurers at heart. And right beside the adventurous gold seekers, were the adventure writers. Authors like Alexandre Dumas, Mark Twain and Bret Harte came to spin romantic tales of life in the hills outside Sacramento.

Mark Twain was certainly one of the wittiest, brightest and most audacious of all writers. He came to the mining country in 1864 to see the action for himself, and he stayed to write about it. He even had visions of finding the great Mother Lode himself and he did have minor success with silver. Myths, visions and dreams were all he took East with him, though, including the moment that he was a millionaire. Twain described his near miss:

"But just suppose some person were to tell you that two thousand dollar ledges were simply contemptible – contemptible, understand – and that right yonder in sight of this very cabin there were piles of pure gold – oceans of it – enough to make you all rich in twenty-four hours! Come!!

"I should say he was as crazy as a loon!' said old Ballou, but with wild excitement, nevertheless.

"'Gentlemen,' said I, 'I don't say anything – I haven't been around, you know, and of course don't know anything – but all I ask of you is to cast your eye on *that*, for instance, and tell me what you think of it!' and I tossed my treasure before them.

"There was an eager scramble for it, and a closing of heads together over it under the candlelight. Then old Ballou said: 'Think of it? I think it is nothing but a lot of granite rubbish and nasty glittering mica that isn't worth ten cents an acre!'

"So vanished my dream. So melted my wealth away. So toppled my airy castle to the earth and left me stricken and forlorn.

"Moralizing, I observed, then, that 'All that glitters is not gold.'"

And what happened to men like John Sutter and James Marshall, California's first gold miners? Mark Twain's moral could be their epitaph. Sutter's huge land holdings were overrun by prospectors, who snatched gold from under Sutter's very nose. Futile petitions to Congress for restitution netted him nothing. He died destitute in 1880. James Marshall died a broken-down, penniless, alcoholic, weepy old man in 1885, on the site of his original findings.

The perennial problem to the miners was women – or, more accurately, the lack thereof. They would go to any lengths just to catch a fleeting peek at a woman. Mark Twain visited a decayed mining camp in Toulumne, California, and came back with these descriptions:

"In those days miners would flock in crowds to catch a glimpse of that rare and blessed spectacle, a woman! Old inhabitants tell how, in a certain camp, the news went about early in the morning that a woman was come! They had seen a calico dress hanging out of a wagon down at the camping ground – sign of emigrants from over the great plains. Everybody went down there, and a shout went up when an actual, bonafide dress was discovered fluttering in the wind! The male emigrant was visible. The miners said:

"'Fetch her out!'

"He said: 'It is my wife, gentlemen – she is sick – we have been robbed of money, provisions, everything, by the Indians – we want to rest.'

"'Fetch her out! We've got to see her!'

"'But gentlemen, the poor thing, she –'

"'FETCH HER OUT!'

"He 'fetched her out,' and they swung their hats and sent up three rousing cheers and a tiger; and they crowded around and gazed at her, and touched her dress, and listened to her voice and with the look of men who listened to a *memory* rather than a present reality – and then they collected twenty-five hundred dollars in gold and gave it to the man, and swung their hats again and gave three more cheers, and went home satisfied."

Twain goes on. "And while upon this subject I will remark that once in Star City, in the Humboldt Mountains, I took my place in a sort of long, post office single file of miners, to patiently await my chance to peep through a crack in the cabin and get a sight of the splendid new sensation – a genuine, live Woman! And at the end of half of an hour my turn came, and I put my eye to the crack, and there she was, with one arm akimbo, and tossing flap-jacks in a frying pan

with the other. And she was one hundred and sixty-five years old, and hadn't a tooth in her head. (Being in a calmer mood now, I voluntarily knock off one hundred years.)"

The men that history remembers best are those who made their fortunes supplying the miners. Philip Armour was a butcher and he sold the miners meat. Armour's meat market prospered. In five years he made $8,000 – enough to move to Milwaukee to create an empire of packing and slaughtering houses that became the foremost meat supplier in the entire nation.

Armour had a friend in the Gold Rush country by the name of John Studebaker. John and his brothers had built a modest carriage works in Indiana. But John was restless. With $68 in his pocket, he migrated to California and began making a one-wheeled cart to carry rock and ore out of the mining country. He called it a wheelbarrow. He also saved $8,000 in five years and returned to Indiana, where he and his brothers built their carriage works into the famous and successful Studebaker Wagon Works.

And then there was Levi Strauss, a canny supplier who carved a very special niche for himself. He sailed from New York in 1850 with a stock of cloth that he sold on board the ship. All except one bolt of canvas, that is. As he stepped off the ship he met a miner who needed a pair of trousers and Levi Strauss was in the pants business. Soon, he developed a special rivet that stengthened the seams in his pants and from that time on, Levi's were known as the most durable trouser – able to withstand the test of wear, hard use and time. Strauss soon employed 500 workers and grossed about one million dollars a year.

Although men's fortunes skyrocketed to dizzying heights with the discovery of gold, it was the state of California that reaped the major benefits. From a sleepy little muddy village of 450 in 1847 before the gold rush, San Francisco grew to a bustling town of 50,000 by 1860. The population of the entire state grew to 300,000. Businesses to supply all these folk sprang up everywhere. The fertile Central Valley yielded up lush vegetables and grains. The California cattle herds grew from 260,000 to 3 million in 10 years.

As the wealth of California increased, so did the need to transport people and goods from the more populous Eastern states. Mail was particularly important. Railroads were reaching their spidery fingers up and down the East Coast and as far out as St. Louis, but that was where they stopped.

Finally, in 1857, Postmaster General Aaron Brown awarded a contract to John Butterfield, one of the founders of American

Express, to carry mail and passengers twice a week from St. Louis and Memphis to San Francisco. At last the West Coast would be linked to the East.

It was a complicated contract, though. Instead of traveling due West, following the route traveled by most of the covered wagons, Butterfield was required to travel a Southern route, going through Tucson, Arizona and Los Angeles before reaching San Francisco. This added about 800 miles to the trip and considerable danger as well. And Apache Indians hated to be disturbed!

Cries of scandal and scheming followed this contract. Brown said he chose the Southern route to avoid the harsh winters of the North, but no one believed him. Mail and passengers could actually reach California faster by way of Panama! The *Chicago Tribune* called the contract "One of the greatest swindles ever perpetrated upon the country by the slave-holders." And there was the crux of it. All issues were either pro- or anti-slavery. This was clearly a battle won by the slave states.

Butterfield met all obligations of his contract. He bought 100 Concord coaches, 1,000 horses, 500 mules and used 800 men to travel the 1800 miles. Good organization allowed him to shave 48 hours off the required time of 25 days.

Nevertheless, competition was inevitable. It came in the form of a massive advertising campaign called the Pony Express. Eighty young riders, traveling in relay, could speed the mail across the Northern route in a mere 10 days. But, although the derring-do caught the imagination of the public, another invention would soon make the Pony Express obsolete. The Pony Express began operations in April, 1860. Three months later, Congress authorized the construction of a telegraph line from the Missouri frontier to California. By October, 1861 the Pony Express was dead.

Butterfield was still doing well when, in 1861, the newly elected President, Abraham Lincoln, decided to move his operation from the explosive Southern states to the Northern route. Finally, Butterfield was operating along the preferred route. The only question was how long that would last. With the Southerners out of Congress, a bill was passed authorizing a railroad that would reach clear to California.

The railroad was inevitable, so rather than fight it, Butterfield joined it. By selling out his interests to Wells Fargo, feeder lines were created that brought goods to the railheads for shipment across the country.

California's gold rush had been remarkably free of greed and violence. But, as the gold became scarce, tempers flared and men's willingness to live compatibly side by side diminished. Competition increased, along with licentiousness, theft, greed and violence.

With the rise of lawlessness came the actual outlaws themselves. First, there was Black Bart. He has the distinction of staging the first successful stagecoach robbery in California.

Black Bart was a gentleman through and through. He was a dapper little man with a stylish derby hat, cocked at a rakish angle. He carried a natty little walking stick. There was a diamond pin in his scarf and a handsome diamond ring on his finger. Across his vest he wore a heavy, gold watch chain. He had deep, bright-blue eyes, a large, gray mustache, neatly trimmed and waxed and a meticulously trimmed beard. As he walked, he smiled a good-natured, satisfied smile. He loved his home in San Francisco.

Black Bart plied his trade on the stagecoach runs between the gold mines of the Mother Lode and the Coast. He had a great sense of humor. During his robberies he wore a flour sack over his head which baffled lawmen for years. The eyes just seemed too far below the top of his head. Later, it was suspected that he wore his derby under his flour sack to make it seem as if he were taller.

When conducting a robbery, Black Bart always spoke in a soft, well-modulated voice. He would say: "Throw down the box." No one ever argued because he used a double-barreled shotgun to back up his demand. Courtously thanking the driver, Black Bart would send him on his way. Later, when authorities returned to inspect the scene of the crime, they found the Wells Fargo box empty except for a poem signed by "Black Bart, the PO 8." (poet)

Six years went by and Black Bart held up twenty-seven Wells Fargo stages. He never wounded or hurt anyone and, one time, when a terrified passenger voluntarily tossed him her purse, he bowed politely and handed it back to her saying, "Madam, I am interested only in the Wells Fargo box and the United States Mail."

Nevertheless, the career of Black Bart was about to come to an end. One day in 1883, Black Bart stopped a stage out of Sonora. As usual, he commanded, "Throw down the box." But Wells Fargo was getting smarter. They had riveted the box to the floor. So Black Bart ordered the driver down and forced open the box.

But before Black Bart could escape with his loot, little Jimmie Rolleri, who had been out shooting rabbits, came upon the scene and quickly saw what was happening. He and the driver were friends so he handed over his gun. With that, Black Bart felt a sharp pain right in the rump. It didn't take him long to head for the hills, leaving a trail of blood behind.

Actually, that wasn't all Black Bart left behind. The posse found a sack Bart had cached that contained all kinds of clues to his identity. The one that did him in, however, was a handkerchief with a San Francisco laundry mark. Detectives traced it to Black Bart. He was sentenced to six years but got out in four and one-half due to good behaviour. Or, perhaps they let him out so they wouldn't have to put up with any more of his poems. The last one credited to him makes the point:

"I rob the rich to feed the poor,
Which hardly is a sin;
A widow ne'er knocked at my door
But what I let her in.
So blame me not for what I've done,
I don't deserve your curses,
And if for any cause I'm hung,
Let it be for my verses!"

An outlaw of an entirely different sort was a man by the name of Tiburcio Vasquez. He was a buck-toothed, murderous little cutthroat of a bandito. Although he became a folk hero to his Mexican countrymen, he had a long career as a cattle rustler, stagecoach robber and murderer. He was convicted of murder in 1876 and hanged.

The gold rush had lasted a mere five years for the forty-niners. By then, hordes of men had stripped the land of the last small grain of gold dust. Gone were the days of crouching beside a mountain stream. Now it was up to the men of industry. They knew there were giant streaks of gold embedded deep in the earth. To extract it, they banded together and dug shafts, creating efficient mining operations. Some of the larger operations would continue for many years, but for most men it was as good as over by 1853.

And then silver was discovered. During the gold rush, men had been bothered by a gluey, bluish clay at a spot on the slopes of the Sierra near Lake Tahoe. There was gold embedded inside, but they had a terrible time getting it out. The heavy clay seemed to be everywhere and it clogged the sluice-boxes, making them inoperable.

Then one day in 1859 a drifter by the name of Henry Comstock came along and stumbled onto a gold-bearing strike being worked by James Finney and Manny Penrod. For reasons thoroughly lost to history, these two agreed to share their stake with Comstock. Maybe it was because they were

doing so well. With the batch of gold they sent to Grass Valley, California to be assayed, they sent along some of that blue clay. Much to their surprise, they found that it was rich in silver – almost $4,000 worth.

Comstock retired from mining then and there. But he devoted an enormous amount of time to perpetuating the myth that he, and he alone, was responsible for the silver rush. Comstock died in the traditional fashion – broke; but his name lives on, associated with the greatest of fortunes.

Some did strike it rich. The Consolidated Virginia Mine, in the Comstock, regularly disgorged $6 million monthly. By 1863, $40 million of silver had been taken out of the ground and by 1880, roughly 20 years after the first great find, the total yield had reached the dizzying heights of $400 million.

Properly speaking, the Comstock Lode was in Nevada.

Politically, financially and commercially, however, it clearly belonged to California. Supply routes and mined silver traveled by way of California. The Comstock was owned by Californians and its impact changed the face of California.

Socially, the "Silver Kings" became titans of San Francisco society, building grand homes on Nob and Russian Hills. Financially, the Comstock was responsible for the creation of California's first stock exchange. It created a demand for new types of machinery to probe the depths of the earth, and thus was born the state's heavy manufacturing industry.

The Comstock Lode transformed San Francisco from a sleepy little town to a sophisticated city. Billy Ralston, the Comstock's largest owner, plunked all his holdings right back into the city. William C. Ralston symbolized the strutting self-confidence of the frontier city. He was brash, energetic, and resourceful. He had arrived in San Francisco in 1853, a bit too late for the Gold Rush, but he didn't let that stop him.

Ralston came to California as agent for a New York steamship line. When they opened a bank, Ralston learned the business through and through. Soon he left the steamship line and formed his own bank. He called it the Bank of California and opened branches in Virginia City and other towns just becoming flushed with the wealth of silver. As the Comstock mines brought larger and larger deposits to Ralston's banks, Ralston amassed great personal wealth and he invested in the mine himself.

Ralston loved California with a passion. He poured his Comstock earnings into sugar refineries, lumber, stage and water companies, a transcontinental railroad and America's largest city hotel.

The Palace Hotel had been a special dream of Ralston's for years. He knew exactly what it would look like and where he would put it. Now, in 1872, he bought a plot of land on Market Street in San Francisco, hired an architect and sent him East to study the great hotels on the East Coast. On the architect's return, the two men sat down to make their plans.

The hotel would cover an entire city block, with a spacious central court that would supply light and air to the interior rooms. It would rise to a height of seven stories and contain bands of bay windows. The interior courtyard would be capped by a vaulted dome of glass.

Ground was broken early in 1873, and by spring of 1875 it was clear to all of San Francisco that this was going to be the grandest hotel in America. It had all the latest conveniences, including electric clocks on all floors, gaslighting, electric call buttons in each room, air conditioning, hydraulic elevators and "tubular conductors" to carry mail and small parcels throughout the building. It even had a series of artesian wells and water towers to serve as its own fire department in case of fire.

As the scaffolding was removed from the exterior, a profusion of bay windows, white walls and gold trim was revealed. A reporter from *Leslie's Illustrated Newspaper* in New York visited the building and said: "Striking as is the vastness of the building when viewed from a point near at hand, to get a true idea of it's comparative size one must see it from the Bay, east of the city. Viewed from this standpoint, it is the most conspicuous object in the view and looming up above the sea of houses, presents a grand and imposing appearance."

"The furnishing of the hotel," wrote another visiting reporter, "has been attended to in a style corresponding with the magnificence of the building. The greatest care has been given to selecting furniture, upholstery, table-ware, bedclothing and everything necessary to throw the charm of a luxurious and refined home around the spacious rooms and stately halls. Marble, rosewood, and ebony, elaborately carved and polished, gleamed throughout the building, and the walls of the public rooms, painted a delicate shade of pink, blush like the cheek of a peach."

The grand opening was set for October 14, 1875. It took place as scheduled, but without Billy Ralston. With no governmental insurance to back up bank resources, banks were often subject to demands or panics by groups of depositors who could withdraw their funds at will.

The 1870s saw one of the worst depressions California has known. The losses in the Comstock mines were tremendous. Finally, a run on "Black Friday", August 26, 1875 caused Ralston to slam shut the huge oaken doors of the Bank of California. The next day he was found floating in San Francisco Bay.

Had he lived, he would have been proud of his Palace Hotel. In time, the list of Palace notables read like a roster of the great of the age. They included Rockefeller, Morgan, Carnegie and Pullman, Henry Ward Beecher, Carrie Nation and the Prince of Siam. Rudyard Kipling and Oscar Wilde were guests, as well as Judge Oliver Wendell Holmes and Presidents Hayes, Harrison and Mckinley. The railroad tycoon, Leland Stanford, occupied a suite at the northeast corner of the hotel while his forty-room mansion on Nob Hill (now the site of the Stanford Court Hotel) was being built. The "Divine" Sarah Bernhardt moved mountains of baggage into an eight-room suite at the Palace in 1887, and in 1894 Eugene Sandow, the world's "most perfect physical specimen", appeared in pink tights in the Palace's Maple Room, where he flexed his biceps, expanded his chest and invited reporters to punch him in the stomach.

Another big winner in the Comstock Lode experienced a fate far different from Ralston's. His name was George Hearst. He was one of the early investors in the Comstock mine. But there was a difference between Hearst and Ralston. Hearst took his money out of the Comstock and invested it in the famous Homestake Mine in Lead, South Dakota, still the largest gold mine in the world.

Hearst and his wife Phoebe built a grand house on Nob Hill, where they entertained lavishly. They passed along a vast fortune to their son William Randolph Hearst, who went on to found the *San Francisco Examiner* and finally the vast network of Hearst Publishing.

Mining wasn't the only way for a man to get rich in California. "The Big Four", as they were known, consisted of Charles Crocker, Leland Stanford, Mark Hopkins and Collis Huntington. They all lived in Sacramento, where Crocker was a dry-goods clerk, Stanford a grocer and Huntington and Hopkins dealt in hardware. At least they did until they invested in the scheme of a young engineer named Theodore Dehone Judah. It was his idea to build a railroad that would link the West Coast to the East. The government helped things along nicely when they granted huge tracts of land to the railroad as right of way.

It never occurred to folks that these huge land grants would drive the price of agricultural land to shameful heights. Nor did it occur to anyone that the importation of "Crocker's Pets," the hundreds of thousands of Chinese laborers who helped build the railroads, would eventually lead to racial tension.

The railroad, known as the Central Pacific and later the Southern Pacific, made The Big Four insanely rich. They saw nothing wrong in squeezing young Judah out at an early stage.

In 1868, five years after construction began, the first Central Pacific train crossed the Sierras at Donner Pass. Thirteen months later, on May 12, 1869, the Golden Spike was driven at promontory Point, Utah and the two coasts were linked forever.

Leland Stanford learned so much about political maneuvering while working to build the railroad that he took up politics as an occupation. He served as Governor of California and as a Senator in Washington.

"The Big Four" eagerly built enormous mansions up on Nob Hill to display their wealth. Crocker's mansion stood where Grace Cathedral now rises; the Hopkins abode, where the Mark Hopkins Hotel now stands; the Huntington home was where the Huntington gardens are now located and, as mentioned earlier, the Stanford mansion was located on the present site of the Stanford Court Hotel.

The Stanfords were plain, quiet folk. They built a home reflecting their dignified good taste. The greatest disappointment of their lives was when their son died on a family trip to Italy. Stanford told his wife at the time, "The children of California shall be our children." So, together, they founded Leland Stanford Junior University and endowed it richly. Unfortunately, Stanford died two years after the university was founded and then a depression hit. Jane Stanford wasn't sure how she was going to meet the expenses of the university.

So, Jane became more and more frugal, barely spending anything on herself. She sold several houses and tried to sell all her jewels. Slowly, bit by bit, she kept improving the magnificent university that now enjoys such world acclaim. When she died she left a fine endowment that has helped to sustain its excellence.

Mark Hopkins wanted a simple residence similar to the Stanford's. But Hopkins' wife was twenty years younger and had very different ideas. She pleaded and teased and finally Hopkins agreed to let her build whatever she wanted on the half lot adjoining the Stanford's.

What she built became one of the most amazing houses ever built in San Francisco. It was of wood painted to imitate stone. It had towers and turrets and verandas and porticos and a Gothic glass conservatory. It had wings with towers of bay windows. It was a lurid imitation of a French castle, combining Gothic and Greek and Arabic and Provencal architecture. There was even a baronial dining room that could seat sixty guests and a master bedroom that imitated a room from a Venetian palace. Its walls were of ebony inlaid with precious stones and with intricate designs of ivory. The inner doors were padded with rich blue velvet and there were cupids painted on the ceiling. In total dismay, Mark Hopkins called this monstrosity the "Hotel de Hopkins".

Fortunately for Hopkins, he never had to live there and neither did Mrs. Hopkins. Hopkins died before the house was finished and his widow moved East. She found she really enjoyed housebuilding so she hired a prominent young architect and had him build her a half-dozen mansions on the East Coast. Then she married him, disinherited her son and left her entire fortune to her new husband. You can imagine the uproar that caused!

Even as Mark Twain was learning that "All that glitters is not Gold", so were those along California's northern coast. Some things were just gold of a different color. They called it green gold. We call it timber. Lumber is still big business in Northern California.

The cathedral-columned redwood is the world's tallest living plant. One is reputed to have reached more than 369 feet into the sky. Logging is a tortuous, back-breaking chore, especially since most of the California timber is in mountainous country and has to be transported to the coastal towns for shipment by boat or barge.

Roads were "impassable, not even jackassable" most of the winter. The rivers weren't much better. One sage quipped: "Of all the variable things in Creation, the most uncertain are the actions of a jury, the workings of a woman's mind, and the conditions of California's rivers. The crookedness you see ain't but half the crookedness there is."

Nevertheless, by the end of 1849, sawmills were springing up just north of San Francisco in redwood country. Cities like Mendocino and Eureka played important roles in the development of the West. Their lumber built cities in the West and East. Technology was developed to make loading and unloading easier, and special ships, suitable for carrying the massive lengths of lumber, were designed.

It cannot be denied, however, that early lumber barons were

wasteful and negligent. More lumber than was used was left on the ground to rot. This, in turn, was set ablaze to leave the earth scorched and raw.

One observer noted: "Nothing is more appalling than the sight which greets the eye upon emerging suddenly from the tall, stately green redwoods upon the scene of desolation which follows the logger. The whole country is a blackened, charred mass. The very soil has been burned and shows the result of intense heat. Every living green twig, every vestige of life has been wiped out."

Eventually, dedicated conservationists convinced forest products firms and government agencies that conservation was a sound idea. It was necessary to preserve the natural beauty and made good sense economically. Today, much of the Redwood Country is preserved in National Forests where lumbering is permitted, but only if forest management practices are observed.

Thankfully, the redwoods that remain today are majestic wonderlands – awesome in their grandeur. Garborville is a charming place to view them first-hand. A stay in the Benbow Inn, with its elegant, antique dining room, its intimate bar, quaint rooms and broad veranda filled with wicker chairs and tables, is relaxing. And a trip north through the Avenue of the Giants should not be missed.

Eureka is a city built on lumber. But, even with one of the heaviest concentrations of Victorian homes anywhere in America, the Carson House is a standout. With its peaked roofs and gables and hodge-podge of architectural trim, nothing could possibly embody the effervecence and light-hearted spirit of Victoriana more.

Scenic wonders abound in California. From Eureka it's an easy trip to Mt. Shasta, a big, white, ice-cream cone of a mountain. Just to the south lies one of California's largest lakes, Lake Shasta. Created by the damming of the Sacramento River, it is a popular resort for fishing, hiking, camping and boating.

In fact, the majesty of the Northern California coast is breathtaking in its entirety. It twists and curves its tortuous route from sheer rocky cliffs to scenic beaches, all the way from Fort Bragg on the north to Big Sur on the south.

Big Sur is as much a feeling as a place. It's as if going there, almost to the ends of the world, one can communicate directly with God. The cliffs plunge into the sea and the surf roars and beats the rocks into sand, except in the secluded coves of utter calm, where the sea gently washes the sand and sandcrabs scuttle across the open beach. It's a desolate area, almost devoid of homes. The only indication one gets of a residency is an occasional mailbox. Few roofs or roads dot the landscape. The occasional cry of a gull or the barking of a sea lion is often the only sound to interrupt the roar of the surf.

Carmel-by-the-Sea is the jewel in this lovely landscape. No neon signs, garish gas stations, stoplights or even streetlights mar the idyllic village. Instead, it's filled with cozy little cottages and tree-lined streets that have the peaceful calm of an 18th century European village. Antique and craft shops have small wooden signs announcing their wares. Even restaurants and inns only reveal themselves in small signs and menus outside their doors. No fast-food franchises, high-rise buildings or used-car lots mar the landscape. Instead, plazas, courtyards and mews lead to charming inns, art galleries, outdoor cafes and bookstores.

San Francisco has much of similar nature. Union Street, Ghiradelli Square, Fisherman's Wharf, The Cannery – all are graced with lovely outdoor cafes, stores and bookshops – but with a difference. Where Carmel offers subdued quiet – a peaceful hideaway – San Francisco treats the visitor to lively action. Street musicians entertain, seagulls screech overhead, ships blow their horns in the harbor and America's only moving National Landmark, the cable cars, clatter up and down the steep hills.

Today, elegant stores line Union Square downtown and culture abounds, with resident companies in opera, symphony, ballet and theater. Traveling Broadway shows make San Francisco a regular stop. Up the hill in Pacific Heights, elegant mansions line the streets.

But gone are the mansions of Nob Hill, including those of Huntington, Crocker, Stanford and Hopkins, and no story about Northern California could be complete without relating why.

It was early in the morning – 5:12, to be exact – on April 18, 1906. San Franciscans were jolted out of bed by a tremendous trembling of the earth. It was an earthquake. Windows broke, dishes fell, cornices tumbled into the streets and the brand new City Hall just crumbled to dust. Miraculously, no one was killed.

But, just as San Franciscans were assessing the damage, they noticed billows of black smoke and an eerie light in the sky coming fron the financial district. A series of small fires had joined forces and was marching forth. By mid-afternoon the financial district was destroyed. San Francisco was primarily a wooden city and it became a tinderbox. Ralston's magnificent Palace Hotel on Market Street was engulfed.

Residents fled to the hills, where they lived in hastily erected sheds or tents, while the fire raged for three days and nights. In the end, over four-fifths of the city had been destroyed – amounting to more than $400 million. And over 200,000 people were without homes.

One of the most graphic exhibits of the destruction the fire wrought can be viewed in the halls just off the main lobby of the Fairmont Hotel. It's worth a trip just to see the exhibit.

San Franciscans didn't let a fire stop them, though. They rebuilt quickly, and this time they used bricks and mortar. They even took the precaution of building artesian wells into street intersections to provide a ready source of water in case of another fire. In a matter of days, signs were sprouting up announcing: "On this site will be erected a six-story office building to be ready for occupancy in the fall." This renaissance created the San Francisco we know today.

A renaissance of a different sort had been going on for some time just to the north of San Francisco, and, unlike the gold from the Mother Lode, the gold from this renaissance just gets more and more plentiful.

It all started when a nobleman from Hungary decided to take a trip to America. The year was 1840 and the young man had not been prepared for what he found. "My God," he wrote, "how many people are in utter misery in Europe, unable to provide their meagre needs whereas here nature offers just for the taking millions of acres of rich black soil which just needs to be turned over to produce a bountiful harvest..."

He returned to Hungary with visions of rolling green and gold fields. There, he convinced his father to liquidate the family estate. He sold his wife's dowry and they had a fairly substantial sum. So, in the fall of 1842, Count Agoston Haraszthy, his wife and three small children and his father and mother moved to America.

But just before making the move, Haraszthy published the diary he had used on his first American journey. It was titled: *Travels in North America* and it was extensively reviewed by the European press. This little book had quite an impact. It encouraged other Europeans, frustrated at the difficulties of making a living in Europe, to move to America.

The Haraszthys settled in Wisconsin and Agoston immediately went about the business of organizing a city. He built roads and bridges and homes and churches. He built a boat to ease transportation and he organized an emigrant society to help emigrants settle in their new land. He did alright by himself too, by selling land and goods to the new settlers.

He is still spoken of in Wisconsin in almost heroic terms. This description was printed in 1906. "He was an arresting figure; a large active man, very dark with black hair, wide black mustache and full black beard. His dark eyes reflected the moods of a dreamer and a doer. He loved to ride hard and hunt game. He seemed born to command, yet his friends found him generous to a fault. He was of a poetic disposition and was a brilliant conversationalist."

The family stayed in Wisconsin a mere six years and then struck out for California. This seems to have been due to a search for a warmer climate. They settled in San Diego, where both father and son became active in local politics, but Agoston continued other pursuits as well.

In Wisconsin he had become convinced that, in the right climate and with the right soil, fine European grapes could be grown. These grapes, he believed, were capable of producing wines to equal those produced in France, Germany and Italy.

He grew a few grapes in Southern California that he had ordered from Europe, but he was disappointed. The climate was too warm. He often complained that his vines didn't get their proper rest due to the lack of winter.

By 1851, Haraszthy had been elected to the state legislature. That took him north to Vallejo and, during breaks in the legislative session, he spent his time searching for better wine-growing land. He bought land just north of Mission Delores in San Francisco and built a lovely estate. But grapes didn't grow well here either. The summers were too cool and foggy. He restlessly moved his vines and 20,000 of his choice fruit trees to Crystal Springs in San Mateo County. They did better here but he still wasn't satisfied.

By this time Haraszthy had settled on his plan to grow the grapes of his native Europe and to make fine wines in this new country. He was convinced it could be done. All he needed was to find the right combination of sun, soil and rain.

From cuttings he received from another Hungarian living in the United States, Haraszthy was still experimenting. It is widely thought that one of the original cuttings from Hungary included the famous mystery grape – the Zinfandel. No one is quite sure where it came from but it is today the most widely planted red wine grape in California.

Haraszthy planted another grape from his Hungarian cuttings that was equally impressive. The Muscat of

Alexandria was planted in Crystal Springs and was the foundation for California's major raisin growing industry.

Then one day Haraszthy made a visit to General Mariano Guadalupe Vallejo, north of San Francisco in Sonoma. Vallejo had been growing Mission grapes for over 20 years and was considered the leading California vintner. Vallejo's wines were unimpressive; Mission grapes were noted only for the poor quality wine they produced.

It was Vallejo's land that impressed Haraszthy. The valley had rich soil, bathed in warm sun, with rolling, sheltered hills protected from the fog of San Pablo Bay, and as an added plus, it was remarkably close to the grape market in San Francisco. The wind currents and general topography reminded him of his native Hungary.

Land was cheap in Valley of the Moon, and soon Haraszthy owned more than 6,000 acres. Within a few years, he had planted over 400 acres with grapes. Unlike Vallejo, Haraszthy planted his vines on the slopes of hills, rather than in the valley where they could be close to rivers and streams. This made him the first to demonstrate how effectively grapes can grow on non-irrigated land.

Haraszthy named his estate Buena Vista (beautiful view) and built one of the finest houses in the entire Bay area. It was a white, Pompeiian style building with exquisite formal gardens in the front, enclosed by an ornamental fence.

Right in sight of the magnificent mansion, the vineyards were growing steadily. In 1857 alone, Haraszthy planted 80,000 vines on 118 acres. In addition, he encouraged his friends to settle near him to try their hand at grape growing too. His friends included Charles Krug, Emile Dreser and Jacob Grundlach, who each made significant contributions of their own to the fledgling wine industry.

Haraszthy built his first winery in 1857 too. He built it of native stone to blend with the landscape and then complemented the winery by extending tunnels into the limestone hillside behind, that could serve as a cool, year-around storage cellar. This was ideal for wine that demanded a constant temperature.

The shortage of oak to make barrels to age the wine didn't trouble Haraszthy too much. He experimented with redwood and found that it was a suitable replacement. Today, redwood is used almost exclusively by California vintners.

By this time, Haraszthy was winning prizes for his wine right out from under the nose of General Vallejo. The two men had maintained a friendly, competitive spirit ever since Haraszthy had arrived. They shared new techniques and vines. Their friendship was cemented forever when, in 1863, Attila and Arpad Haraszthy married the beautiful twin daughters of General Vallejo.

But Haraszthy's contribution to the wine industry was just beginning. In 1861 he convinced the California State legislature to send him to Europe to bring back cuttings from the finest vineyards. He and his son Arpad, who had been studying the technique of champagne manufacturing in France, wound their way across the vineyards of Germany, Italy, France and other important wine producing regions.

On his return, Haraszthy drafted a report to the legislature that said: "I have purchased in different parts of Europe 100,000 vines, embracing about 1,400 varieties and small lots of choice almonds, olives, figs, pomegranates, Italian chestnuts, oranges and lemons – enough to propagate by grafts." In one short span of five months, Haraszthy had imported the products from a thousand years of wine and fruit culture in Central, Western and Mediterranean Europe to California.

Regrettably, the legislature failed to follow Haraszthy's recommendations for distribution of the vines. Some were lost, and many of them died. But, production at Buena Vista just kept improving. The first casks of Zinfandel were ready in 1862 and they were even better than had been hoped. Larger storage cellars were built to accommodate increased production.

All this success didn't go unnoticed. In fact, it was William Ralston, from the Bank of California, who in 1863 proposed to Haraszthy that the Bank take over his mortgages to help him raise capital for further expansion.

Haraszthy was interested in expanding into champagne production, and he looked on this offer as the ideal opportunity. He could use new capital. So, Ralston created a corporation, with Haraszthy as manager of the winery.

Things got off to a great start until the champagne production took a turn for the worse. Impatient with experimentation, Ralston ordered Haraszthy to cease the champagne line. This was Arpad's pride and joy. Rather than stop production, Arpad left the corporation and started production on his own in competition. It grew to be a huge success.

This didn't sit well with Ralston. In anger, he finally forced the father out of the corporation that he had so lovingly fostered.

The year was 1866. What would Haraszthy do now? He had an indomitable spirit and seldom allowed setbacks to stop him, but he felt his usefulness at Buena Vista had come to an end. And he was tired of fighting.

He was fifty-six years old, but he had the spirit of a man in his twenties. He decided to try something totally new. So, he, his wife and son Geza, sailed for Nicaragua. There, he bought a sugar plantation and built it into the largest in the country. Next, he built a rum distillery and was granted an export monopoly.

And then calamity struck. In 1868, Eleonora Haraszthy came down with yellow fever and died. And, early in 1869, on a trip to Nicaragua to see his son, the father died too. That was in January. By July, Agoston himself was dead. His body was never recovered, so the actual cause of death is unknown, but it is generally assumed that he was eaten by an alligator while surveying his land.

One of his children wrote the following account: "About the middle of the stream a large limb was found to be broken and at the same place, a few days before, an alligator dragged a cow into the stream from the bank. We must conclude that father tried to cross the river by the tree, and that losing his balance he fell, grasping the broken limb, and then the alligator must have drawn him down forever."

He was eulogized throughout California. In fact, as recently as 1969, on the 100th anniversary of his death, the United States Congress entered the following in the Congressional Record: "... Too often we overlook those true men of vision whose foresight has so profoundly influenced our lives... California has put Count Haraszthy on its cultural maps and there is no doubt he belongs there. In a very significant way he put California on the nation's economic and gourmet maps..."

But, that's only part of the California renaissance, of course. Another renaissance of tremendous proportions has been underway since the 1930s. In fact, the development of the Silicon Valley actually had its genesis in 1899. That's when folks in San Francisco received the first ship-to-shore wireless message, and the electronics industry was born. In 1909 the first scheduled radio station started broadcasting from San Jose and that was the same year that the first American radio firm was founded. It was located in Palo Alto.

Then, in 1938, two recent Stanford graduates, David Packard and William Hewlett, founded an electronics firm in their garage in Palo Alto. From that small beginning the huge Hewlett-Packard firm, now one of the world's largest makers of electronic testing equipment and computers, was born.

The first computers used vacuum tubes to amplify and transmit sound. That was revolutionary in its day, and in the 40s the first digital computer was built. It used 18,000 vacuum tubes. Then, at Bell Laboratories, the transistor was invented. It could do what the vacuum tube had done, but was only the size of a pea. In 1957 the integrated curcuit followed. This tiny "chip" could contain thousands of transistors.

One thing led to another and the computer age was born. As principals of one company formed a new one, spinning off new products and technology, support firms grew up in close proximity. Research facilities, venture capital firms and colleges sprouted in the Silicon Valley.

Thirty years ago San Jose was a sleepy town surrounded by prune trees. Today, it is almost the size of San Francisco, and is the fastest growing city in America. That creates all sorts of problems. Housing is almost impossible to find, and rush hour traffic clogs the inadequate highways and produces a dense brown smog that creates a pall over the landscape.

And yet, the Silicon Valley has a sense of magic to some. It's today's quest for gold, in all respects like the rush for gold in the Mother Lode. But the gold today is in the form of a little micro chip. It's a place of hot tubs, Mercedes Benzes and inventions that are obsolete by the time they hit the market.

But Californians like to move fast. And they play as hard as they work. So it's not surprising that on weekends there's a general rush for a vacation retreat. For many that might be Lake Tahoe, one of the truly magnificent spots on earth. It's a mere 200 miles from San Francisco to Tahoe, where hiking trails, hidden lakeshore caves and snow-covered backroads lure city folk. Nearby, ski resorts offer snowy challenges and, just across the border in Nevada, casinos offer challenges of another sort.

So, just as in the rest of California, Tahoe is a study of contrasts. The high-rise hotels and casinos give way, just across the California border, to thick forests of trees, emerald coves for fishing and beaches for sunning. The most active environmental groups in the nation are positioned side by side with the biggest environmental polluters.

Maybe O. Henry said it best: "East is East, and West is San Francisco, according to Californians. Californians are a race of people; they are not merely inhabitants of a state."

Previous page: a felled giant in Calaveras Big Trees State Park, east of Sacramento, shows the massive bulk of these trees. It is the huge sequoias (overleaf) which are the most sought after and popular features of Kings Canyon National Park, east of Fresno, but the tumbling waters (these pages) which carved the canyon have a beauty and majesty all their own.

Kings River, which forms the heart of Kings Canyon National Park, is surrounded by towering peaks and sheer cliffs: (above) Horseshoe Road and (facing page) the Grand Sentinel. Overleaf: Yosemite National Park is one of the most spectacular areas in California: (left) the cascading Vernal Falls and (right) sunset gleams on the face of Half Dome as it stands above the valley.

These pages and overleaf: Yosemite National Park, between Modesto and the Nevada border, contains some of the finest scenery in California. These pages: the white cascade of the Upper and Lower Yosemite Falls. Overleaf: (left) El Capitan and the Merced River and (right) Cathedral Rocks.

The distinctive face of Half Dome features in both views (these pages) of Yosemite National Park; (above) from the banks of the tranquil Merced River and (facing page) from the mouth of the Wawona Tunnel. Overleaf: (left) fishermen on the still surface of Silver Lake in the High Sierras and (right) the Dana River becomes a torrent with the melting snows of spring.

g page: a cattle ranch north of Bridgeport, near the Nevada border, where the heavy winter snows often
 roads impassable. Above: a traditionally clad cowboy shows that traversing the High Sierras is often best
 on horseback. Overleaf: (left) a car stirs up dust in Sonora Pass, one of the routes near Bridgeport
 is often closed in winter, and (right) nearby Mono Lake and its surrounding mountains.

35

The Olympic Valley Inn (previous pages left) which lies to the north of the D.L. Bliss State Park, on the shores of Lake Tahoe (previous pages right and facing page). Above: the curious inlet on Lake Tahoe known as Emerald Bay. Overleaf: (left) the clear, green waters of Lake Tahoe at D.L. Bliss State Park and (right) a stern-wheeler glides past Fannette Island in Emerald Bay.

Previous pages, facing page and overleaf right: the boat-studded waters of Emerald Bay surround the ruin-topped Fannette Island. Above: a beautiful, sandy beach near Tahoe Keys. Overleaf left: trees and undergrowth cling precariously to the rugged mountain slopes above Emerald Bay.

ag page: the stern-wheeler *Tahoe Queen*, which travels the length and breadth of Lake Tahoe, takes on
engers at South Lake Tahoe. Above: small craft on the sandy beach at South Lake Tahoe. Overleaf: (left)
 Street in South Lake Tahoe and (right) yachts moored in a marina at Tahoe Keys on the south shore of Lake
e.

51

Above: picnickers take advantage of the facilities at Eldorado Beach on the shores of Lake Tahoe. Facing page:
the cable car which ascends the Eagles Nest and offers superb views across the 22-mile-long Lake Tahoe.
Overleaf: (left) the crystal-clear waters at sandy Eldorado Beach and (right) the frothing waters of Eagle
Falls cascade down towards Emerald Bay.

Above and top: the ten block section of Old Sacramento which has been restored and renovated in keeping with its gold rush origins. Top left and left: views along Capitol Mall. Facing page: the majestic dome of the State Capitol, completed in 1874. Overleaf: (left) a ship glides between fertile fields near Sacramento and (right) the Capitol from the air.

Above: grain fields and (facing page) sheep grazing in the Delta Valley, south of Sacramento. Overleaf: (top left) the Firehouse, (bottom left) Broad Street and (right hand page) Main Street, all in the old gold-mining center of Nevada City, northeast of Sacramento; (top center) the Old City Hall and (top right) the Firehouse in Auburn, south of Nevada City; (bottom right) the Empire Mine in Grass Valley.

Between 1914 and 1921 a series of eruptions occured at Lassen Peak in northeastern California, though today the volcano has settled down somewhat. Lassen Volcanic National Park, which covers some 163 square miles around the peak still shows the effects of volcanic and thermal activity, as at the steaming springs and boiling mud pools in Bumpass Hell (these pages and overleaf).

The sign reads:

DANGER
MUD POTS, FUMAROLES
AND POOLS ARE VERY HOT
GROUND CRUST MAY BE
THIN OR SLIPPERY
STAY ON TRAILS

Lassen Volcanic National Park has much to offer the visitor at all times of the year: (above) the road curving beneath Mount Lassen; (facing page) a tumbling stream near the Sulfur Works Thermal Area; (overleaf left) snow-spattered Mount Conrad and (overleaf right) Boiling Lake in Bumpass Hell.

ng page: the incredibly delicate tracery of the Burnley Falls, east of Enterprise. Above: the forest and ng land of the Mount Shasta - Fall River area. Overleaf: (left) the Camden House, near Redding, built in by Charles Camden and (right) boats in the Brandy Creek Marina, on Whiskeytown Reservoir.

Top left: the Glory Hole in Whiskeytown Reservoir, west of Redding. Remaining pictures: the magnificent, sandy beach at Brandy Creek, which draws sunbathers and swimmers from far and near during the summer. Overleaf: (left) Lake Shasta, which was created by the construction of the massive dam (right).

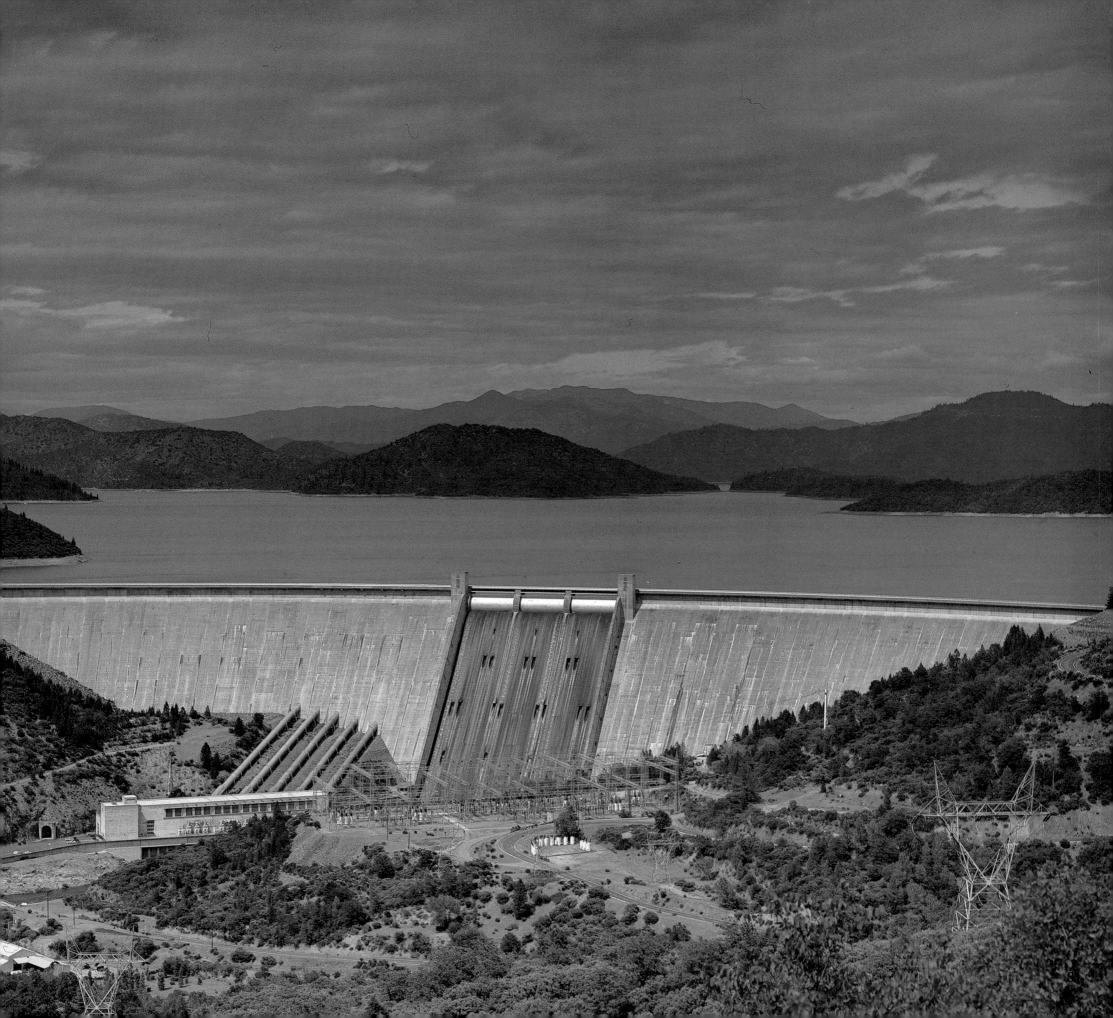

e pages and overleaf left: the 14,161-foot-high mass of Mount Shasta rises above the countryside north of
ng. Overleaf right: the impressive heights of Castle Crags which lie south of Dunsmuir. The crags were
d out of 200 million-year-old granite by the forces of erosion and given their final shaping during the
ges in the last million years.

Previous pages: the waters of Lake Siskiyou which draw both bathers and yachtsmen alike. These pages: the rugged landscapes and sparse vegetation of the Lava Beds National Monument near Tule Lake, the result of extensive lava flows in the past few thousand years. Overleaf: (left) Mount Shasta and the boulder-strewn bed of Gumboot Creek and (right) the Klamath River seen from State Highway 96.

ng page: an automatic irrigation device waters fields near Tulelake. Above: pelicans at rest on a nearby
. Overleaf: (left) coastal fog rolls in towards the mountains in the Redwood National Park and (right) the
bird Johnson Grove of coast redwoods, the tallest living things in the world.

Previous pages: (left) a truck carrying logs crosses the Klamath River near Weitchpec and (right) the river in less gentle mood. Above: a view of the coast from the Klamath Overlook. Facing page: part of the two mile row of fishermen's campers which borders United States Highway 101 south of Klamath. Overleaf: (left) two examples of the massive redwoods near Klamath and (right) Point St. George, just ten miles south of the Oregon state line.

BIG TREE

HEIGHT	304	92.6
DIAMETER	21.6	66
CIRCUMFERENCE	68	20.7
ESTIMATED AGE	1500 YRS.	

SHRINE
DRIVE-THRU TREE

| 5000 | HEIGHT 275 FT. |
| 21 FT. | CIR. 64 FT. |

MYERS FLAT, CALIFORNIA

Above: the small building which serves as the lighthouse at Trinidad, north of Eureka. Facing page: the sun sinks below the Pacific horizon south of Eureka. Overleaf: yachts and working vessels moored in the Woodly Island Marina in Eureka, the most important port between San Francisco and the Columbia River.

Previous pages: (left) the Burl Sculpture at Benbow; (center) one of the huge redwoods near Leggett and (right) Eureka's 2nd Street. These pages and overleaf: scenes near Yuba City; (top left, top right and facing page) the rich grain harvest; (above) a plaque at Sutter Buttes; (right) thinning peaches in the orchards and (overleaf) the grazing land east of Yuba City.

ATTENTION PUBLIC
LIFEGUARD ON DUTY
AT THIS BEACH FROM
10 A.M. TO 6 P.M. DAILY
PARK COMMISSIONER CITY OF LAKEPORT
NO SWIMMING
OR
DIVING
FROM
PIERS OR FLOATS

CF 3235 HP

199

113

Previous pages: (left) Clear Lake near Konocti; (top center) a lifeguard by Clear Lake; (bottom center) Port Sonoma Marina; (top right) Clear Lake State Park and (bottom right) Lake Mendocino. Top left: Christian Brothers Vineyard, (above) Berlinger Brothers Vineyard and (top right and facing page) nearby scenes, all around St. Helena. Left: the home of General Mariano Guadalupe Vallejo, founder of Sonora. Overleaf: vineyards near Healdsburg.

These pages: landscapes around Healdsburg. Overleaf: (left) a view from Chimney Rock in Point Reyes National Seashore and (right) the unspoilt beach of Gray Whale Cove, north of Montara.

Above: perched high on its lonely crag, Point Reyes Lighthouse is a well known feature of the coast north of San Francisco. Facing page: the majestic sweep of the Golden Gate Bridge, which was opened in 1937 amid great controversy as to whether or not it marred the beauty of the Bay. Overleaf: (left) the pyramid Transamerica Building and the skyline of San Francisco and (right) a cargo ship entering the Bay.

Above: Chinatown, a 16-block area of San Francisco which contains the largest Chinese population outside Asia. Its many shops, restaurants and buildings all reveal their Chinese connection. Facing page: evening gloom draws in on the beautiful Golden Gate Bridge. Overleaf: farmland near Livermore, east of San Francisco.